Geology Rocks!

Igneous Rock

Rebecca Faulkner

Raintree

Chicago, Illinois

Editorial: Melanie Waldron and Rachel Howells
Design: Victoria Bevan
and AMR Design Ltd (www.amrdesign.com)
Illustrations: David Woodroffe
Picture Research: Melissa Allison and Mica Brancic
Production: Duncan Gilbert

Originated by Chroma Graphics Pte. Ltd
Printed and bound in China by
South China Printing Company

11 10 09 08 07
10 9 8 7 6 5 4 3 2 1

Library of Congress Cataloging-in-Publication Data:

Faulkner, Rebecca.
  Igneous rock / Rebecca Faulkner.
    p. cm. -- (Geology rocks!)
  Includes bibliographical references and index.
  ISBN-13: 978-1-4109-2747-7 (Library binding)
  ISBN-10: 1-4109-2747-4 (Library binding)
  ISBN-13: 978-1-4109-2755-2 (pbk)
  ISBN-10: 1-4109-2755-5 (pbk)
  1. Rocks, Igneous--Juvenile literature. 2. Rocks--Analysis--Juvenile
literature. I. Title.
  QE461.F354 2007
  552'.1--dc22
                          2006037174

Acknowledgments
The author and publisher are grateful to the following for permission to reproduce copyright material:

Alamy p. **20** (Arco Images), p. **37** (Belinda Lawley), p. **38** (Bernd Mellman), p. **23** (Dianna Bonner Martin), p. **22** (GC Minerals), pp. **5 top inset, 30** (LeighSmithImages), p. **41** (Photo Resource Hawaii); Collections pp. **5 bottom inset, 28** (Colin Inch); Corbis p. **11**, p. **42** (Alberto Garcia), p. **10** (Ashley Cooper), p. **39 bottom** (Bettmann), p. **16** (David Muench), p. **12** (Douglas Peebles), p. **32** (Galen Rowell), p. **4** (Jeff Vanuga), p. **5** (Jim Sugar), pp. **24, 44** (Pablo Corral Vega), p. **35** (zefa/Tony Craddock); GeoScience Features Picture Library pp. **17, 18, 18-19 middle, 33**, p. **19** (Prof. B. Booth); Getty Images p. **43**, (AFP Photo/Edgar Romero), p. **31** (George Diebold), p. **6** (Iconica/Frans Lemmens), p. **35 inset** (National Geographic/Paul Chelsey), p. **26** (Photodisc), p. **15** (Photonica), p. **39 top** (Riser), pp. **5 middle inset, 29** (Stone), p. **19** (Visuals Unlimited); istockphoto.com p. **13** (Maciej Laska), p. **13 inset** (Ralph Paprzycki); Nasa p. **40**, p. **9** (Visible Earth); Photolibrary p. **25**; Science Photo Library p. **27** (Dirk Wiersma)

Cover photograph of Giant's Causeway in County Antrim, Northern Ireland reproduced with permission of Science Photo Library (Lawrence Lawry).

Every effort has been made to contact copyright holders of any material reproduced in this book. Any omissions will be rectified in subsequent printings if notice is given to the publisher.

Disclaimer
All the Internet addresses (URLs) given in this book were valid at the time of going to press. However, due to the dynamic nature of the Internet, some addresses may have changed, or sites may have changed or ceased to exist since publication. While the author and publishers regret any inconvenience this may cause readers, no responsibility for any such changes can be accepted by either the author or the publishers.

CONTENTS

Any words appearing in the text in bold, **like this**, are explained in the glossary. You can also look out for them in the word bank at the bottom of each page.

FIERY ROCKS

Learn about rocks

There are more than 600 different types of igneous rocks, but do not worry, you will not be expected to learn about all of them. The study of rocks is called geology. Even a geologist will not know everything about all the rocks on Earth.

Rocks have been around from the start of Earth's history. Some rocks can take millions of years to form. Rocks can also be broken down and destroyed over millions of years. Igneous rocks are the most common rocks on Earth. They are found below most of the ocean floor and make up large areas of the **continents**. Some islands, such as Iceland and Hawaii, are made entirely from igneous rocks.

Igneous rocks are sometimes called firey rocks because the word "igneous" means "made from fire" in Latin. Igneous rocks are not actually made from fire, but are made from very hot **molten** rock that comes from deep inside Earth.

Boar's Tusk is an igneous rock formation in Wyoming. It is around three million years old.

continent large land mass

You may have seen images of volcanoes erupting on television, but did you know that volcanoes produce igneous rock? The **lava** that is thrown out of volcanoes, sometimes very violently, will eventually cool and harden to form igneous rock.

Some volcanoes erupt dramatically, but fortunately for those living nearby, this does not happen very often. Other volcanoes ooze lava almost continuously. Mount Etna in Sicily (an island off the coast of Italy) produces lava almost constantly, with occasional mildly explosive eruptions.

Find out later

What did the Aztecs use igneous rocks for?

What Olympic sport uses igneous rocks?

Where is the "granite city"?

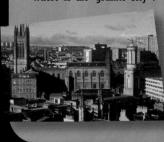

 The lava spewing out of this erupting volcano will harden to form igneous rock.

lava name for magma when it reaches the surface of Earth
molten melted

CRUSTY OLD ROCKS

What's inside Earth?

Igneous rocks begin their life inside Earth, but what is Earth like deep down? The inside of Earth is a bit like an onion. It is made up of different layers.

The **crust** is like the skin of the onion. It is a relatively thin layer covering Earth's surface. There are two types of crust: continental and oceanic. Continental crust is found beneath the **continents** and can be up to 43.5 miles (70 kilometers) thick. Oceanic crust is found beneath the oceans and is thinner than continental crust. It is only about 6.2 miles (10 kilometers) thick, but it is heavier than continental crust.

Digging deeper

Earth's crust is made from rock. We cannot always see this rock because it may be covered with water, soil, or buildings, but it is definitely there. If you dig down deep enough you will see it. Are there any areas near your school where you can see Earth's crust?

Here in Algeria, Earth's crust is not covered with soil or buildings, so we can see it is made of rock.

core central layer of Earth
crust thin surface layer of Earth, made of rock

If we could peel away the onion-skin crust, we would find the **mantle**. This is a thick layer, starting at the base of the crust and extending 1,800 miles (2,900 kilometers) deep into Earth. This is where igneous rocks start their life, but we do not see them until they rise into the crust or gush out of volcanoes on the surface of the crust.

If you could travel deep down into the center of Earth you would find the **core**. The core can be separated into the outer core (which is liquid) and the inner core (which is solid). No one really knows much more about the core because it is too deep for us to study.

Melting rocks

The rocks in the mantle are so hot that they are partly **molten**. Temperatures in the mantle can reach up to 5,400° Fahrenheit (3,000° Celsius). This is still only half as hot as the surface of the Sun.

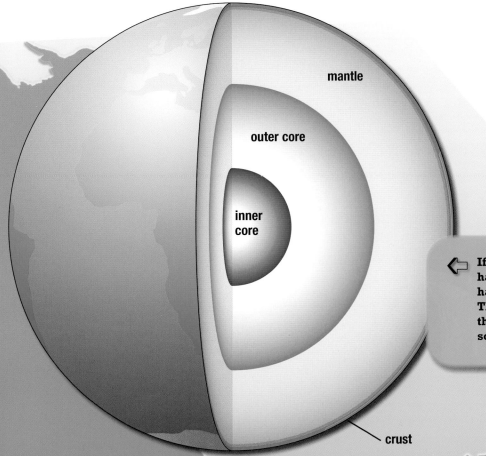

mantle

outer core

inner core

crust

If we could slice Earth in half we would see that it has layers, like an onion. The outer layer of Earth, the crust, is made of solid rock.

Does the crust move?

Earth's **crust** does not form one solid layer. Instead, the crust is broken up into huge, moving pieces called **plates**. These fit together like a giant jigsaw puzzle.

The plates float like rafts on the **mantle** below. They move very slowly over Earth, up to 4 inches (10 centimeters) per year. Although the plates move slowly, they are constantly moving, and carrying the **continents** and oceans with them.

In some places the plates are moving away from each other. This usually occurs along giant mountain chains on the ocean floor, for example the Mid-Atlantic Ridge. This creates a gap (**rift**) between the plates. **Lava** rises up from the mantle to fill the gap, creating new igneous rock.

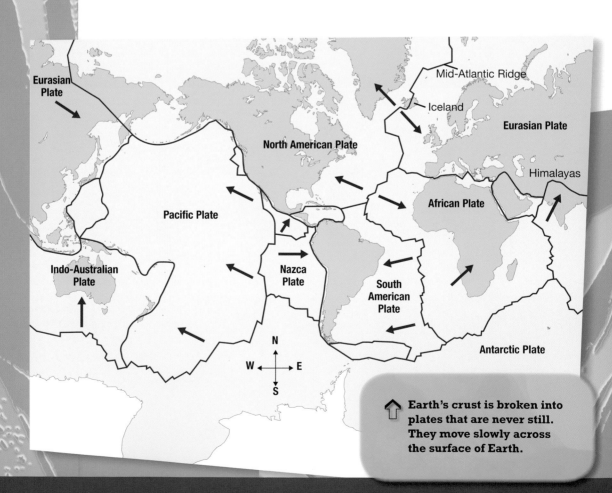

Earth's crust is broken into plates that are never still. They move slowly across the surface of Earth.

plate giant, moving piece of crust

In other places plates are moving toward each other. One plate may slide under the other and plunge into the mantle below, where it melts. Volcanoes often form along this kind of **plate boundary**, for example in the Andes in South America. Sometimes plates may collide or crash into each other. When this happens the crust is squashed and folded at the plate boundary. This can form huge mountains, such as the Himalayas.

Plate tectonics
The slow, continual movement of plates is called **plate tectonics**. The boundaries between plates are known as plate margins.

The Andes mountain chain is shown by the snow-capped peaks on the left. They run down the west coast of South America. The chain contains many volcanoes along the boundary between the Nazca Plate and the South American Plate.

ROCKS AROUND THE WORLD

What are rocks?

Rocks are found all over the surface of Earth. You can find rocks in high mountain ranges, on the sea floor, in river beds, in deserts, under the ice at the South Pole, and even in your yard. If you dig deep enough into the soil you will find rock underneath. The whole of Earth's **crust** is made of rocks.

The rocks that make up Earth's crust are not the same all over the world. There are many different types of rock. It all depends on what the rocks are made of, and the conditions in which they were made.

⬇ Rocks are found everywhere. Sometimes they create amazing landforms like these huge columns on the island of Skye, Scotland.

granite coarse-grained, extrusive igneous rock

All rocks are made of natural substances called **minerals**. There are more than 4,000 different minerals on Earth, but only about 100 of these are commonly found in rocks. The rest are very rare.

A rock may contain many different minerals. The igneous rock **granite** contains the minerals quartz, feldspar, mica, and hornblende. If a rock contains hard minerals, such as quartz, it will be a hard rock. Granite contains lots of quartz, so we know that it is hard.

Cookies and rocks

Rocks are similar to chocolate chip cookies. The cookies are made of flour, butter, sugar, and chocolate in the same way that rocks are made from minerals. You can see the lumps of chocolate in a cookie, just as you can see large mineral grains in a rock.

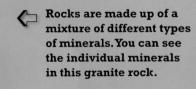
Rocks are made up of a mixture of different types of minerals. You can see the individual minerals in this granite rock.

What types of rock are there?

Common rocks
Granite and **basalt** are igneous rocks. They are two of the most common rocks on Earth. Most of the continental crust is made of granite, and most of the ocean crust is made of basalt.

Earth's **crust** is made up of three groups of rock that are created in different ways:

- igneous rock
- **sedimentary rock**
- **metamorphic rock**.

Igneous rocks are made from hot liquid material called **magma** that is found in the **mantle**. Over millions of years the magma rises up from the mantle and through Earth's crust. As it does so, it cools and hardens to form igneous rock.

This lava has cooled and hardened to form igneous rock. It is called **pillow lava** because it looks like lots of pillows.

magma molten rock from the mantle

Sedimentary rocks are formed from broken pieces of other rocks. When igneous rocks are attacked by wind and rain at Earth's surface, tiny particles are broken off and carried by the wind or in rivers. They are eventually deposited in a new place and build up over millions of years to form new sedimentary rock.

Metamorphic means changed. Metamorphic rocks are formed when heat or high **pressure** changes igneous or sedimentary rocks. When hot magma rises below Earth's surface it heats up the surrounding igneous rocks, like baking them in an oven. This causes the rocks to change into metamorphic rocks. When mountain ranges form, the rocks are squashed and buried under the growing mountains. This means they will experience high pressure, so they will change into metamorphic rocks.

Sedimentary rocks

In areas where pieces of mud and clay collect, they form a sedimentary rock called **shale**. In areas where sand collects, it forms a sedimentary rock called **sandstone**.

This building is made from marble. Marble is a metamorphic rock formed when limestone is heated.

This rock outcrop is formed from sandstone. Sandstone is a sedimentary rock made from sand grains.

The rock cycle

On Earth there is an unending cycle of rock formation, break down (**weathering**), transportation (**erosion**), and settlement in a new place (**deposition**). All these processes make up what is called the **rock cycle**.

As soon as igneous, **sedimentary**, and **metamorphic rocks** are exposed at Earth's surface, they are attacked by wind and rain. This is called weathering and, over millions of years pieces of rock are chipped away.

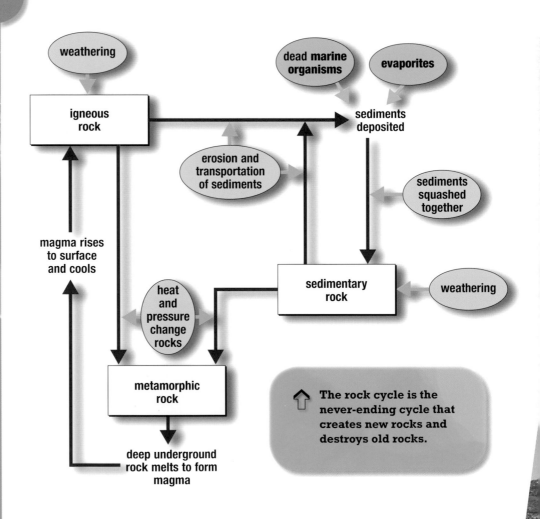

The rock cycle is the never-ending cycle that creates new rocks and destroys old rocks.

deposition laying down weathered rock in a new place
erosion removal and transportation of weathered rock

Some of these pieces of rock are small enough to be carried away to different places by wind, rivers, or ice. This is called erosion. When they can be transported no further, the pieces of rock (sediment) are dumped in a new place. This is called deposition. Over millions of years, this deposited sediment changes into new rock, and the cycle can begin all over again.

In areas where **plates** collide, igneous and sedimentary rocks will be put under intense **pressure** and heat. Over millions of years, they will change into metamorphic rock. In turn, the metamorphic rock may be heated so much that it melts to become **magma**. This magma may then rise and solidify to form igneous rock once again.

The oldest rocks
Earth is at least 4.5 billion years old but, as rocks are continually being destroyed, there are no rocks left that are this old. The oldest rocks that have been found on Earth are found in Canada and are 3.9 billion years old.

◁ These huge **granite** boulders, called the Devil's Marbles, are found in Australia. They are formed as layers of granite have peeled off due to weathering and erosion.

INGENIOUS IGNEOUS ROCKS

How are igneous rocks formed?

Igneous rocks are formed as **magma** rises from the **mantle** and cools in Earth's **crust**. Magma can cool either underground or at Earth's surface, both on land and underwater.

We know that rocks are made of **minerals**, and minerals grow as crystals. When magma cools and hardens to form igneous rock, this is called **crystallization**. If magma cools slowly underground, there is plenty of time for large crystals to form. This means the rock produced will be **coarse grained**. Igneous rocks that form underground are called **intrusive rocks**, because the magma intrudes (pushes into) the crust.

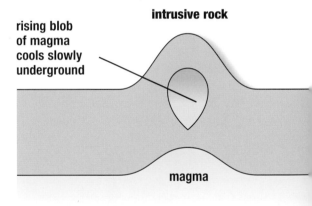

intrusive rock

rising blob of magma cools slowly underground

magma

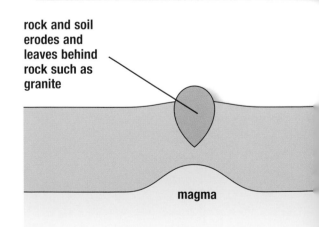

rock and soil erodes and leaves behind rock such as granite

magma

⇨ Igneous rocks are formed when magma cools underground (intrusive rocks) or at the surface of Earth (extrusive rocks).

extrusive rock igneous rock that forms on the surface of Earth

When magma rises all the way to Earth's surface it is called **lava**. Sometimes this lava erupts onto the surface of the crust through volcanoes. Once on the surface, the lava cools quickly, so there is little time for crystals to develop before the rock hardens. This means the crystals will be small, and **fine-grained** rock such as **basalt** is formed. Igneous rocks that form on the surface of Earth are called **extrusive rocks**.

Tiny grains
Sometimes the crystals in extrusive igneous rocks are so small you need a microscope to see them. Rhyolite (below) is a fine-grained rock formed when lava cools quickly at Earth's surface. You cannot see any individual mineral grains in this sample because they are too small to see without a microscope.

extrusive rock

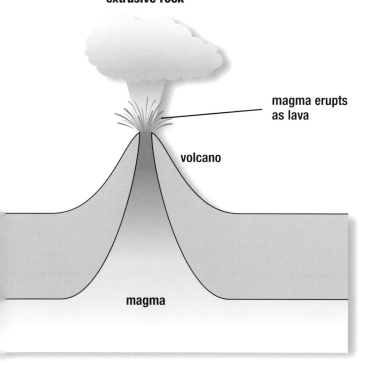

magma erupts as lava

volcano

magma

lava cools to form rock such as basalt

magma

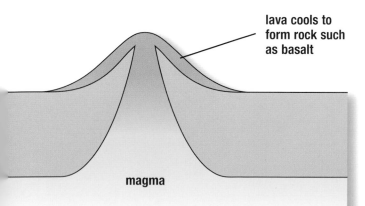

How can we classify igneous rocks?

We can classify (group) igneous rocks according to:

- grain size
- **minerals** present
- color
- texture.

Grain size

Igneous rocks can be **coarse grained** or **fine grained** depending on whether they form deep in the **crust** or at the surface of Earth. We can classify coarse-grained rocks as those containing crystals that are larger than 0.2 inches (5 millimeters) across. Fine-grained rocks are those that have smaller crystals of less than 0.4 inches (1 millimeter) across. Rocks with crystals in between these measurements are medium grained.

Rocks can be classified according to the minerals they contain. This lump of granite contains mainly quartz and feldspar, with small amounts of mica and hornblende.

quartz

accessory mineral mineral found in a rock in tiny quantities

Minerals present

Igneous rocks can also be grouped according to the main minerals they contain. For example, the igneous rocks **granite** and rhyolite can be grouped together because they contain the minerals quartz, feldspar, mica, and hornblende. **Gabbro** and **basalt** can be grouped together because they both contain the minerals plagioclase and pyroxene. All these rocks may contain small amounts of other minerals as well, but they are classified according to the main minerals they contain.

Accessories

Additional minerals found in igneous rocks that are not used to classify them are called **accessory minerals**. Granite may contain the accessory minerals magnetite, garnet, zircon, or apatite. In rare cases pyroxene minerals are also present.

feldspar

mica

hornblende

Color

Igneous rocks can range in color from white **granite** to black **obsidian**, with all shades in between. The color of a rock depends on the **minerals** it contains. A rock containing few dark minerals will be pale in color. The more dark minerals the rock contains, the grayer or blacker it will appear.

Texture

The **texture** of a rock depends on the shape of the individual crystals that make up the mineral grains, and how these fit together. Rocks can be **coarse**, medium, or **fine grained**. Sometimes all the minerals will be roughly the same size, but sometimes there may be a mixture.

This is not a lump of glass, it is obsidian. Obsidian is a jet black, glassy, **extrusive** igneous rock.

vesicle gas bubble in a rock

Texture	Description		Example
phaneritic		rocks are made entirely of large crystals	**granite**
aphanitic		rocks are made entirely of small crystals	**basalt**
porphyritic		rocks are fine grained, but contain a few large crystals set within the fine-grained background	**andesite**
glassy		rocks cool so quickly that there is no time for crystals to form and so they look like glass	**obsidian**
vesicular		rocks contain lots of holes (**vesicles**), formed by gas bubbles becoming trapped in **lava** when it hardens into rock	**pumice**

This Rock, That Rock

Types of igneous rock

The following rocks can be divided into groups according to the main **minerals** they contain.

Granite, pegmatite, rhyolite, pumice, and obsidian

The main minerals found in these rocks are quartz and feldspar. They may also contain the minerals mica and hornblende.

Granite is an **intrusive** igneous rock with large crystals. It is therefore **coarse grained**, due to slow cooling underground. It is usually pale pink or pale gray in color and may sometimes contain very large crystals of feldspar.

Time to grow

Pegmatite is a very coarse-grained intrusive igneous rock. It takes millions of years to cool and solidify underground, so there is plenty of time for the crystals to grow.

Pegmatite has large crystals that are easy to see without a microscope. It can sometimes contain large crystals of gems such as topaz and beryl.

Rhyolite is an **extrusive** igneous rock formed from volcanic **lava**. It has small crystals and so is **fine grained**. Sometimes the crystals are so small you cannot see them, so the rock is glassy. Although it is a fine-grained rock, it often has a few large crystals of feldspar or quartz embedded in it. Rhyolite is usually pale gray.

Obsidian is an extrusive igneous rock. It is black and glassy. You cannot see any crystals because it forms from lava that cools very quickly on the surface of Earth's **crust**.

Floating rocks
Pumice is a frothy looking extrusive igneous rock. It looks frothy because it is full of gas bubbles called **vesicles**. These vesicles make pumice so light that it can float on water. It is the only rock that can do this.

⬇ Although pumice can float on water, eventually it will become waterlogged as the vesicles will fill up with water, and so it will sink.

Diorite and andesite

The main **mineral** found in **diorite** and **andesite** is feldspar. They may also contain hornblende, biotite, and pyroxene.

Diorite is an **intrusive** igneous rock. It is **coarse grained** and is usually speckled black and white.

Andesite is **extrusive** and is formed as **lava** cools at the surface of the **crust**. It is a **fine-grained** rock, but may contain large crystals of feldspar. Andesite can sometimes be so fine grained it appears glassy, and it may contain **vesicles**.

Gabbro and basalt

The igneous rocks **basalt** and **gabbro** look very different, but they are both made from the same minerals. The reason for the different appearance is the rate of cooling. Basalt is an extrusive igneous rock, whereas gabbro is intrusive. Gabbro cools much more slowly than basalt so it contains much larger crystals.

⬇ This volcano is called Cotopaxi. It is just one of many volcanoes in the Andes mountain chain.

The main minerals found in gabbro and basalt are feldspar and pyroxene. They may also contain hornblende, biotite, and quartz.

Gabbro is an intrusive igneous rock with large crystals. It is therefore coarse grained, due to slow cooling underground. It is usually dark gray or black in color.

Basalt is an extrusive igneous rock, formed when lava solidifies at Earth's surface. It is fine grained, but may contain large crystals of feldspar. It is a black rock and, like andesite, may sometimes be glassy or contain vesicles.

⬆ **The Giant's Causeway in Northern Ireland is formed from hexagonal columns of basalt. The basalt is from an ancient lava flow, and the columns form when the rock cools and fractures. There are about 37,000 columns, and they range from 16 to 20 inches (40 to 50 centimeters) across.**

How can we identify igneous rocks?

You may have seen beautiful and amazing igneous rocks in museums, or pictures of them in books like this, but how would you feel if you actually found one yourself? Would you know what it was?

Every day you will see rocks of all shapes and sizes. You can find rocks in your local park, by the sides of roads, or in fields and woods. You can also find rocks on gravestones, steps, your house, or your school buildings.

Scientists examining lava on the side of a volcano.

thin section thin slice of rock, looked at under a microscope

It is not always easy to tell if a rock is igneous or not. You will need to look at the rock closely to see if you can see the **mineral** grains. If the rock is **coarse grained,** it is most likely an igneous rock that formed underground. If you cannot see any crystals in the rock, then it probably formed very quickly, for example when **lava** cooled quickly at Earth's surface.

When scientists want to find out what type of rock a sample is, they take very thin slices of the rock, called **thin sections,** and examine them under a microscope. When the rocks are magnified in this way, we can see the individual minerals they contain. Scientists can study these and use their knowledge to discover what kind of rock it is.

⬆ This is a thin section of andesite. If you looked at an outcrop of this rock, you would not be able to see the crystals because they are too small. By looking at the rock under a microscope, scientists can see what minerals it contains.

Bathroom geologist

Take a look around your bathroom at home. You may see some different types of rock. Try to discover if any of them are igneous. There may be a pumice stone on the side of your bathtub. Pumice is used to smooth rough skin. It is amazing to think that this rock came from a volcano.

BUILDINGS AND BLING

How do we use igneous rocks?

Now that you know what igneous rocks look like, you can look for how they have been used by people in many different ways. You may see **granite** buildings in historic cities, **pumice** stones on the side of your bathtub, an **obsidian** bracelet in a jewelry shop, or a granite work surface in your kitchen.

Granite is used on the outside of buildings, such as the Empire State Building in New York City. It is also used for statues and steps because it is hard and **durable**. This means it will be resistant to **weathering** and **erosion**, so will last a long time. The large grains and interesting colors make granite beautiful, and it is also resistant to spills and heat. It is therefore cut and polished to make work surfaces for kitchens and bathrooms.

The granite wall

Parts of the Great Wall of China are made from granite. This 4,500 mile- (7,300 kilometers) long wall is the longest structure ever built. It was built more than 2,000 years ago to keep invaders out. The fact that parts are still standing today shows the resistance of granite.

⬇ Many of the buildings in Aberdeen in Scotland are made of granite. The city has the nickname "the granite city."

durable resistant to weathering

Basalt is also a hard, durable rock. It is used for things such as parking lots and roads because it can withstand the **pressure** of cars continually driving over it. Some of the earliest uses of basalt included the making of ax heads and sculptures.

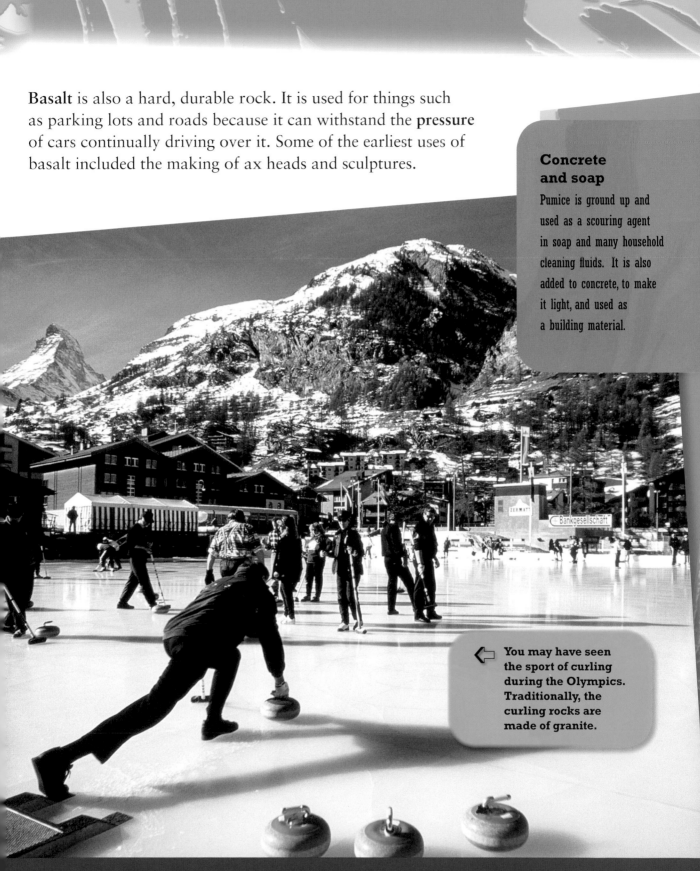

Concrete and soap
Pumice is ground up and used as a scouring agent in soap and many household cleaning fluids. It is also added to concrete, to make it light, and used as a building material.

You may have seen the sport of curling during the Olympics. Traditionally, the curling rocks are made of granite.

Obsidian is used to make ornaments and jewelry, especially earrings, bracelets, and necklaces. This is because its glassy surface makes it shiny and beautiful. In the past it was used for making tools and weapons, such as arrowheads, because it breaks into very sharp pieces.

Diamonds form deep in the **mantle** and are found in a type of igneous rock called kimberlite. Diamond is the hardest substance known, and so is used to make cutting tools. Diamonds are also cut and used in jewelry because the cut surfaces reflect light and make the diamond sparkle.

⇩ **An obsidian arrowhead.**

extract remove from something

We can find **metal ores** in many igneous rocks. Metal ores are mixtures of **minerals** that contain useful metals. These ores can be **extracted** from the underground rocks by mining. The metals can then be separated from the ores and used for many different things. For example, gold and platinum can be used for jewelry, and copper can be used to make pipes and wires.

Diamond drills

The drill a dentist uses to drill teeth is made from diamonds. Because diamonds are so hard, the drill will easily wear away tooth particles as it spins at high speeds.

⬆ **This ring is made from platinum with a large diamond set in it. Both the metal and the diamond come from igneous rocks.**

LANDFORMS OF INTRUSIONS

Intrusive igneous landforms

Intrusive igneous rocks are rocks that cool and harden under the ground. As **magma** rises into the **crust** and cools, it forms huge domed lumps of intrusive igneous rock called **plutons**.

Batholiths and tors

Although plutons form underground, they appear at the surface of Earth in some places where the soil and rocks above have been worn away. When large plutons become exposed at the surface of the crust they are called **batholiths**.

The underworld

Plutons are named after Pluto, the Roman god of the underworld. The Romans worshipped Pluto as the giver of gold and silver. These metals are mined from underground, so this is how Pluto came to be the god of the underworld.

Sugarloaf Mountain in Brazil is an example of a batholith.

batholith huge lump of intrusive granite rock that has been exposed at the surface of Earth'

Batholiths are enormous intrusions and are usually made of **granite**. The Sierra Nevada Batholith forms much of the Sierra Nevada mountain region in California. An even larger batholith, covering an area of nearly 80,000 square miles (200,000 square kilometers), can be found in the mountains of western Canada.

In places where batholiths are heavily **eroded**, landforms called **tors** are found, such as in Yosemite Valley in California, and Dartmoor in southwest England. Tors look like piles of boulders stacked on top of each other.

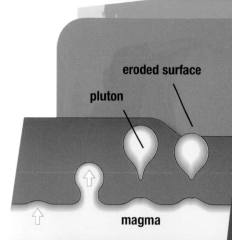

eroded surface

pluton

magma

⬆ Batholiths form as plutons are exposed at the surface due to erosion of the rocks above them.

⬆ This landform is called a tor and is formed from the igneous rock granite. The softer rocks around it have been eroded by wind and rain to leave this unusual rock formation.

Dykes, sills, and plugs

The Great Dyke

The Great Dyke runs 340 miles (550 kilometers) from north to south through the middle of Zimbabwe in Africa. It varies from 2 to 8 miles (3 to 12 kilometers) in width and contains many important metals and **minerals**.

When rocks are **eroded** at Earth's surface, other kinds of igneous intrusions can be exposed, because this rock is much harder. When the top of a vertical sheet of igneous rock appears at the surface of the **crust**, a landform called a **dyke** is formed. The dyke usually cuts across the surrounding rocks and is more resistant to **erosion**, so sticks up.

A **sill** is similar to a dyke, but instead of cutting across the surrounding rocks, the sill lies parallel to them. As the rocks erode, sills usually form cliffs, because sills are also more resistant to erosion than the surrounding rocks.

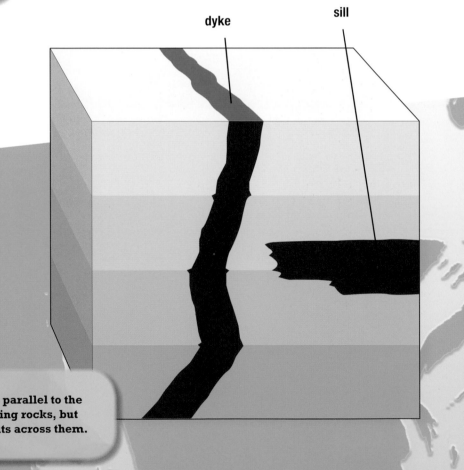

A sill lies parallel to the surrounding rocks, but a dyke cuts across them.

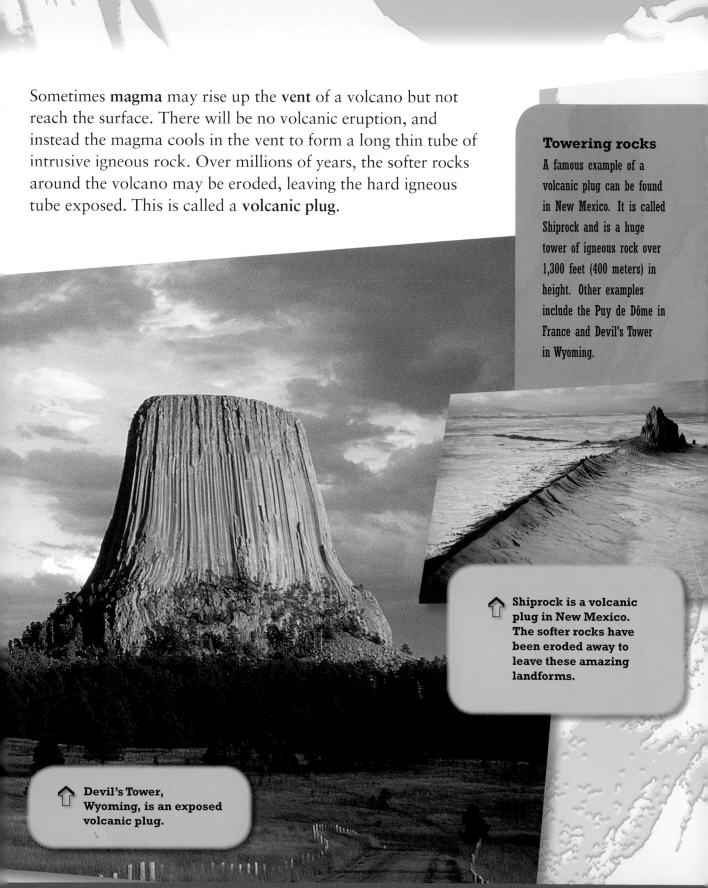

Sometimes **magma** may rise up the **vent** of a volcano but not reach the surface. There will be no volcanic eruption, and instead the magma cools in the vent to form a long thin tube of intrusive igneous rock. Over millions of years, the softer rocks around the volcano may be eroded, leaving the hard igneous tube exposed. This is called a **volcanic plug**.

Towering rocks

A famous example of a volcanic plug can be found in New Mexico. It is called Shiprock and is a huge tower of igneous rock over 1,300 feet (400 meters) in height. Other examples include the Puy de Dôme in France and Devil's Tower in Wyoming.

⬆ Shiprock is a volcanic plug in New Mexico. The softer rocks have been eroded away to leave these amazing landforms.

⬆ Devil's Tower, Wyoming, is an exposed volcanic plug.

volcanic plug long thin tube of intrusive igneous rock that forms when magma cools in the vent of a volcano

LANDFORMS OF EXTRUSIONS

Saving lives
Scientists who study volcanoes are called volcanologists. They try to predict when volcanoes will erupt. Volcanoes do not erupt without warning. Small earthquakes occur and gases are given off when a volcano prepares to erupt. If a volcano is monitored, these warning signs can be seen and many lives may be saved.

Extrusive igneous landforms

Extrusive igneous rocks form when **magma** reaches Earth's surface as **lava**. It then cools and **crystallizes** into rock on the surface.

Mountains of fire

Volcanoes bring magma to Earth's surface. Volcanoes are common along **plate boundaries**. A volcano forms where a break in the **crust** allows hot magma from the **mantle** to rise all the way to Earth's surface. When the magma reaches the surface it is called lava, and the buildup of lava flows over millions of years creates the mountain-like shape of a volcano.

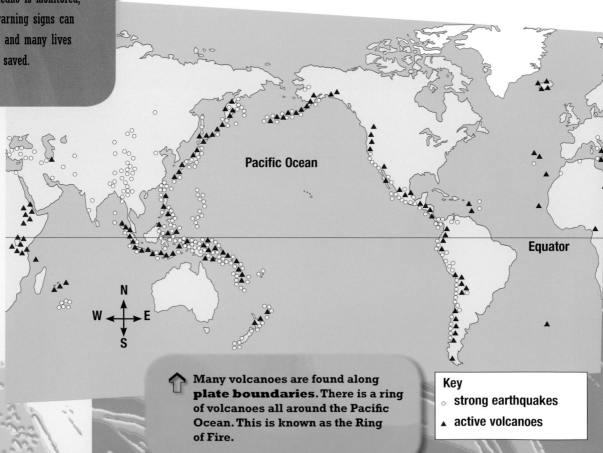

Pacific Ocean

Equator

⬆ Many volcanoes are found along **plate boundaries**. There is a ring of volcanoes all around the Pacific Ocean. This is known as the Ring of Fire.

Key
○ strong earthquakes
▲ active volcanoes

continental flood basalt: huge sheet of basalt lava

The type of landform produced by lava depends on how runny the lava is. **Basalt** lava is very runny. At some points in Earth's history, huge outpourings of flowing lava spread out in enormous sheets over the land surface. These created vast areas of flat land. These huge sheets of lava are called **continental flood basalts,** because they can run out over the land's surface like a flood of water. They are so big they can cover an area bigger than the whole of Texas. In India, a continental flood basalt erupted 65 million years ago, covering half of India.

A flood of basalt

A large area of basalt, called the Columbia Plateau, covers most of the states of Washington and Oregon. More than 300 individual lava flows erupted 16 million years ago to form the plateau. It covers an area of 65,600 square miles (164,000 square kilometers). In some locations, the lava is more than 11,500 feet (3,500 meters) thick.

⬆ This area in India was formed by a massive outpouring of lava.

Underwater lava

There are more than 500 active volcanoes in the world. Most of these are on the ocean floor. Flowing **lava** is produced by underwater volcanoes along mid-ocean ridges. Earth's **plates** move apart at these ridges and, as they do so, lava flows out of the gap in between the plates. This creates new ocean floor. In the middle of the Atlantic Ocean the lava flowing out of the gap builds up to form a long underwater mountain chain, which stretches the entire length of the Atlantic Ocean. This is called the Mid-Atlantic Ridge.

Sometimes so much lava is produced that the ridge sticks up above the ocean surface. This is how Iceland was formed. It is made from lava flows, and it sits right on top of the Mid-Atlantic Ridge.

First parliament

If you go to Iceland you can actually see the Mid-Atlantic Ridge at a place called Thingvellir. This is also the site of the world's first parliament, where ancient leaders were elected and disputes were settled.

➡ Iceland sits right on top of the Mid-Atlantic Ridge, a huge underwater volcanic chain.

a'a lava lava that looks like rubble

As lava cools it becomes less runny and may solidify in different forms. **Pahoehoe lava** looks like a pile of ropes, **a'a lava** looks like the rubble you would find on a building site, and **pillow lava** looks like a pile of pillows.

When **basalt** lava cools, it often fractures into six-sided columns. Because lava flows pile up on top of each other, we cannot usually see basalt columns. When the lava flows are **eroded**, however, amazing landforms—such as the Giant's Causeway in Northern Ireland and the island of Staffa off the west coast of Scotland—can be exposed.

A giant's road

There are many myths and legends associated with volcanoes and igneous rocks. According to one legend, the Giant's Causeway is a road joining Ireland to Scotland that was built by a giant.

⬆ A pahoehoe lava flow in Hawaii (above) and an a'a lava flow in Sicily (right) have now solidified to form igneous rock.

Hot spots

Some volcanoes, such as the Hawaiian islands, are found in the middle of **plates**. How do you think they got there? These volcanoes are created in places where the **mantle** is particularly hot, and manages to break through the overlying **crust**. These are called **hot spots**. Once formed, **lava** leaks out of the hot spot and builds up over millions of years to form a volcano.

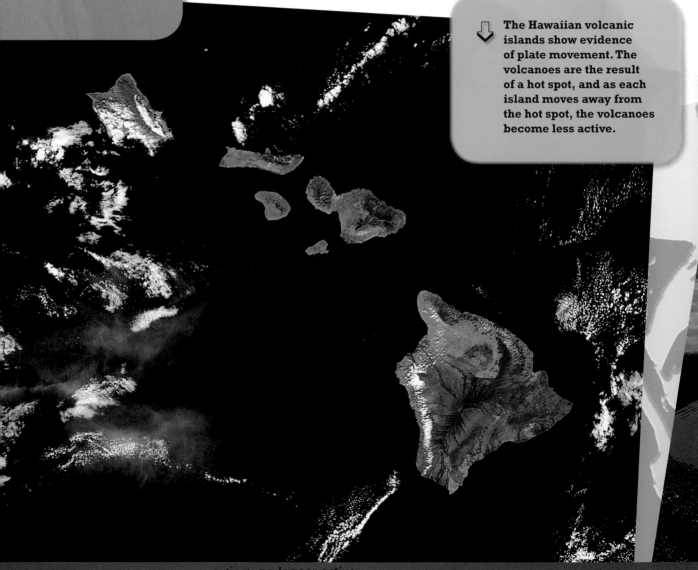

The Hawaiian volcanic islands show evidence of plate movement. The volcanoes are the result of a hot spot, and as each island moves away from the hot spot, the volcanoes become less active.

extinct no longer active
hot spot area where the mantle is particularly hot

The hot spot that formed the Hawaiian Islands is on the floor of the Pacific Ocean. As the lava flows build up they eventually stick out above the ocean surface to form an island. Earth's plates are constantly moving, which means that eventually, over millions of years, the volcanic island will move away from the hot spot, and so the volcano will become **extinct**. A new volcano will begin to form over the hot spot.

The volcanoes of the Hawaiian islands are examples of huge, gently sloping, dome-shaped volcanoes called **shield volcanoes**. They are gently sloping because they are formed from **basalt** lava, which is very runny. It spreads out when it is erupted.

Largest volcano

The largest Hawaiian volcano, Mauna Loa, rises over 29,528 feet (9,000 meters) from the floor of the Pacific Ocean. Not only is Mauna Loa the largest Hawaiian volcano, but it is also the largest volcano in the world.

⬆ Shield volcanoes like this one, called Mauna Kea, in Hawaii, have gentle eruptions, where runny lava flows down the sides of the volcano. Mauna Loa is in the background.

Violent volcanoes

Volcanoes do not only produce **lava**. Many also throw out broken pieces of rock called **pyroclasts**. These range in size from fine particles of ash to volcanic bombs that can be the size of a soccer ball. Some volcanoes are built up over thousands of years from layers of lava and pyroclastic flows. These are called **strato volcanoes**, and they are usually symmetrical.

Sometimes a volcano may erupt so violently that it blows its top off. This forms a **crater** at the **summit** of the volcano. A crater is a bowl-shaped depression. When a volcano becomes **extinct**, a lake often forms in its crater.

Watery volcano

Crater Lake, in Oregon, is a lake in the crater of a volcano. This huge lake is 6 miles (10 kilometers) across and 1,970 feet (600 meters) deep.

⬇ Explosive volcanic eruptions eject huge clouds of ash and devastating pyroclastic flows. This pyroclastic flow was produced in the eruption of Mount Pinatubo in the Philippines, June 1991.

pyroclast rock thrown out of a volcano when it erupts

Huge volcanic eruptions can have devastating consequences for the people living nearby. This is why the work of volcanologists is very important. If they can predict when a volcano is likely to erupt, many lives may be saved.

A volcanic eruption does not have to be violent and powerful to cause a lot of deaths. The 1985 eruption of the Nevado del Ruiz volcano in Colombia was a rather small and insignificant eruption, but 23,000 people were killed. The eruption produced a huge mudslide that completely buried the surrounding towns and villages. If a lot of people live near a volcano, then a lot of people are at risk when it erupts.

Deadly volcanoes

The following are three of the world's most deadly volcanic eruptions.

Year	Volcano	Location	Deaths
1815	Tambora	Indonesia	92,000
1883	Krakatoa	Indonesia	36,000
1902	Pelée	Martinique	28,000

⬆ Some eruptions are so violent that they blow the top off the volcano, leaving behind a crater like this one in El Salvador.

strato volcano volcano built from layers of lava and pyroclastic flows
summit top

CONCLUSION

You can find igneous rocks everywhere. They cover vast stretches of the ocean floor and form many dramatic landforms on the **continents**. They even fly through the air occasionally, in the form of volcanic bombs.

All igneous rocks begin their life as **magma** deep in the **mantle**. Over millions of years this magma rises up into Earth's **crust** or explodes out onto the surface through volcanoes. It then hardens to form igneous rock.

Once at the surface, igneous rocks can create amazing landforms, ranging from flat-lying, hardened lava flows to huge, steep-sided lumps of rock that are the size of mountains.

There are many different types of igneous rock, depending on where they form. Those that form at the surface are usually **fine-grained** and dark in color. Those that form underground are **coarse-grained** and paler.

We have used igneous rocks throughout our history, and still use them today. In the past they were used as tools, weapons, and jewels. Today they are used for lots of things, from buildings to bracelets.

When a volcano starts doing this, you had better get out of the way!

FIND OUT MORE

Books

Bingham, Caroline. *Rocks and Minerals*. New York: DK, 2003.

Harman, Rebecca. *Earth's Processes: Rock Cycles*. Chicago: Heinemann Library, 2006.

Slade, Suzanne. *The Rock Cycle*. New York: Rosen, 2007.

Using the Internet

Explore the Internet to find out more about igneous rock. You can use a search engine, such as www.yahooligans.com, and type in keywords such as:

- batholith
- magma
- pluton

Websites

These websites are useful starting places for finding out more about geology:

Rocks for Kids: www.rocksforkids.com

Rock Watch: www.rockwatch.org.uk

Search tips

There are billions of pages on the Internet so it can be difficult to find exactly what you are looking for. These search tips will help you find websites more quickly:

- Know exactly what you want to find out about first.
- Use two to six keywords in a search, putting the most important words first.
- Be precise. Only use names of people, places, or things.

GLOSSARY

a'a lava lava that looks like rubble

accessory mineral mineral found in a rock in tiny quantities

andesite fine grained, extrusive igneous rock

basalt type of igneous rock formed when lava cools and solidifies

batholith huge lump of intrusive granite rock that has been exposed at the surface of Earth

coarse grained large grains

continent large land mass

continental flood basalt huge sheet of basalt lava

core central layer of Earth

crater circular depression at the top of a volcano

crust thin surface layer of Earth, made of rock

crystallization cooling and hardening of magma to form igneous rock

deposition laying down weathered rock in a new place

diorite coarse-grained, intrusive igneous rock

durable resistant to weathering

dyke vertical sheet of igneous rock that cuts across rocks at the surface of the crust

erosion removal and transportation of weathered rock

extinct no longer active

extract remove from something

extrusive rock igneous rock that forms on the surface of Earth

evaporite sediment left behind as water evaporates

fine grained tiny grains that you need a microscope to see

gabbro fine-grained, intrusive ignous rock

granite coarse-grained, extrusive igneous rock

hot spot area where the mantle is particularly hot

intrusive rock igneous rock that forms underground

lava name for magma when it reaches the surface of Earth

magma molten rock from the mantle

mantle hot layer of Earth beneath the crust

marine organism plant or animal that lives in the ocean

metal ore mixture of minerals that contain useful metals

metamorphic rock rock formed when igneous or sedimentary rocks are changed by heat or pressure

mineral naturally occurring particle. Rocks are made from minerals.

molten melted

obsidian jet black, glassy, extrusive igneous rock

pahoehoe lava rope-shaped lava

pegmatite coarse-grained, intrusive igneous rock

pillow lava lava that looks like pillows

plate giant, moving piece of crust

plate boundary edge of a plate where one plate meets another

plate tectonics movement of the plates across Earth

pluton huge domed lump of intrusive rock under ground

pressure force put on something

pumice extrusive igneous rock that is full of gas bubbles

pyroclast rock thrown out of a volcano when it erupts

rift gap between two plates

rock cycle unending cycle of rock formation and destruction

sandstone sedimentary rock formed from sand grains

sedimentary rock rock formed from the broken pieces of other rocks

shale sedimentary rock formed from pieces of clay

shield volcano dome shaped volcano

sill vertical sheet of igneous rock that lies parallel to the surrounding rocks at the surface of the crust

strato volcano volcano built from layers of lava and pyroclastic flows

summit top

texture how something feels

thin section thin slice of rock, looked at under a microscope

tor eroded batholith

vent hollow tube in a volcano, through which magma rises

vesicle gas bubble in a rock

volcanic plug long thin tube of intrusive igneous rock that forms when magma cools in the vent of a volcano

weathering break down of rock

INDEX